1 MONTH OF
FREE
READING

at

www.ForgottenBooks.com

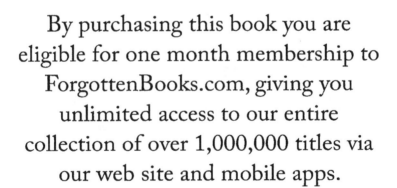

By purchasing this book you are eligible for one month membership to ForgottenBooks.com, giving you unlimited access to our entire collection of over 1,000,000 titles via our web site and mobile apps.

To claim your free month visit:

www.forgottenbooks.com/free1123756

ISBN 978-0-331-43698-3
PIBN 11123756

Forgotten Books is a registered trademark of FB &c Ltd.
Copyright © 2018 FB &c Ltd.
FB &c Ltd, Dalton House, 60 Windsor Avenue, London, SW19 2RR.
Company number 08720141. Registered in England and Wales.

For support please visit www.forgottenbooks.com

The University of
North Carolina

RECORD

The School of Applied Science

FACULTY COMMITTEE ON PUBLICATION OF THE RECORD

ARCHIBALD HENDERSON
JAMES F. ROYSTER
J. G. deR. HAMILTON

PUBLISHED BY THE UNIVERSITY
ENTERED AS SECOND CLASS MATTER AT THE POST-OFFICE
AT CHAPEL HILL, N. C.

CONTENTS

THE UNIVERSITY RECORD
Number 79   Fifty Cents a Year   February, 1910

SCHOOL OF APPLIED SCIENCE

FACULTY

Francis Preston Venable, Ph.D., D.Sc., LL.D., President.
Charles Holmes Herty, Ph.D., Dean.

Walter Dallam Toy, M. A., *Professor of the Germanic Languages and Literatures.*

William Cain, C. E., *Professor of Mathematics.*

Collier Cobb, A. M., *Professor of Geology and Mineralogy.*

Joseph Hyde Pratt, Ph. D., *State Geologist and Professor of Economic Geology.*

Charles Holmes Herty, Ph.D., *Professor of General and Industrial Chemistry.*

Edward Kidder Graham, A. M., *Professor of English.*

Archibald Henderson, Ph.D., *Professor of Pure Mathematics.*

*James Edward Latta, A. M., *Professor of Electrical Engineering.*

Andrew Henry Patterson, A. M., *Professor of Physics.*

William Morton Dey, Ph.D·, *Professor of the Romance Languages and Literatures.*

Alvin Sawyer Wheeler, Ph.D., *Associate Professor of Organic Chemistry.*

James Edward Mills, Ph.D., *Associate Professor of Physical Chemistry.*

Marvin Hendrix Stacy, A. M., *Associate Professor of Civil Engineering.*

Palmer Cobb, Ph.D., *Associate Professor of German.*

James Finch Royster, Ph.D., *Associate Professor of English.*

George McFarland McKie, A.M., *Associate Professor of Public Speaking.*

---

*Resigned, January, 1910.

GEORGE WESTON MITCHELL, *Associate Professor of Drawing.*

JOHN MANNING BOOKER, A. B., *Associate Professor of English.*

OLIVER TOWLES, A. B., *Associate Professor of the Romance Languages.*

THOMAS FELIX HICKERSON, A. M., *Instructor in Mathematics.*

HARRY NELSON EATON, A. M., *Instructor in Geology.*

JAMES MOSES GRAINGER, A.M., *Instructor in English.*

ADOLPHE VERMONT, A.M., *Instructor in the Romance Languages.*

JULIAN COLGATE HINES, JR., S.M., *Instructor in Mathematics.*

THOMAS JOSEPH MCMANIS, *Instructor in Physics.*

COLIN CUTHBERT ALEXANER, A.B., *Instructor in English.*

JONAS MACAULAY COSTNER, A.B., *Instructor in Mathematics.*

CLAUD HOWARD, A.M., *Instructor in English.*

HAMPDEN HILL, S. B., *Instructor in Chemistry.*

EUGENE JOSEPH NEWELL, A.B., *Fellow in Chemistry.*

ERNEST NOELL TILLETT, A. M., *Fellow in Chemistry.*

DUNCAN MACRAE, S.B., *Assistant in Chemistry.*

THOMAS PALMER NASH, JR., *Assistant in Chemistry.*

WILLIAM MERCER OATES, A. B., *Assistant in Chemistry.*

JOHN HILL WHARTON, *Assistant in Chemistry.*

WILLIAM HENRY FRY, *Assistant in Geology.*

FRANCIS EDWARD WINSLOW, A.B., *Assistant in German.*

WILLIAM RUFUS EDMONDS, *Assistant in Physics.*

ALEXANDER LITTLEJOHN FEILD, *Assistant in Physics.*

JUNIUS SPAETH KOINER, JR., *Assistant in Physics.*

†ROYALL OSCAR EUGENE DAVIS, PH.D., *Associate Professor of Chemistry.*

COURSES LEADING TO THE DEGREE OF BACHELOR OF SCIENCE

In order to be recommended for the degree of Bachelor of Science, the student must have passed satisfactory examinations in all the studies required in one of the following courses outlined in this department, I, II, III, IV, and V. Each course combines instruction in certain sciences and their application to the arts with certain other general studies deemed essential to a liberal education.

----

†Resigned, November, 1909.

These courses are designed to furnish the fundamental instruction and to prepare students to pursue the technical professions to which they lead. The courses leading to the degree are five in number; course IIIA. is a special course.

I.   Chemical Engineering.
II.   Electrical Engineering.
III.   Civil Engineering.
      IIIA. Road Engineering.
IV.   Mining Engineering.
V.   Soil Investigation.

ADMISSION

Candidates for admission to the School of Applied Science must present 14 units for entrance. A complete list of these units and the requirements in each subject will be found on pp. 30-36 of the general catalogue.

The specific requirements are as follows:

English *a*, *b*...3. units
History *a* or *b*...2. units
Mathematics *a*, *b*, *c*..3. units
French *a* or German *a*..2. units
Science ....1. unit
Elective..3. units

At least 12 units must be offered. A condition of 2 units may be made up after entrance.

I. CHEMICAL ENGINEERING

FRESHMAN YEAR

English 1...(3)*
Mathematics 1...(4)
German 1..(3)
Chemistry 1...(3)
Drawing 1...(2)

---

*Numerals in parentheses indicate the number of hours a week.

SOPHOMORE YEAR

English 2...(3)
Mathematics 2...(3)
Chemistry 3, Qualitative Analysis..(2)
Chemistry 4, Quantitative Analysis and Assaying.................(3)
Physics 1, General Course...(3)
Drawing 2A...(2)

JUNIOR YEAR

Chemistry 16, Inorganic Chemistry, advanced...................(1½)
Chemistry 2, Technical Chemistry..(3)
Chemistry 17, Quantitative Analysis, advanced..................(3)
Chemistry 5, Organic Chemistry, advanced.........................(3)
Chemistry 7, Elementary Physical Chemistry......................(2)
Geology 1...(3)
Physics 11, Steam Machinery..(1)

SENIOR YEAR

Chemistry 6, Theories of Chemistry.....................................(2)
Chemistry 5A, Organic Chemistry..(2)
Select { Chemistry 7A, Physical Chemistry, advanced.......... (3)
one { Chemistry 7B, Electro-Chemistry........................... (2)
Chemistry 8, Advanced Quantitative Analysis and Research.. (5)
Physics 4A, Electric Machinery.. (2)
Physics 6, Thermodynamics, (fall term) .... (1½)
Geology 2, Mineralogy... (3)

II. ELECTRICAL ENGINEERING

FRESHMAN YEAR

English 1.. (3)
Mathematics 1.. (4)
Select { German 1.. (3)
one { French 1... (3)
Chemistry 1... (3)
Drawing 1.. (2)

SOPHOMORE YEAR

English 2.. (3)
Mathematics 2.. (3)
Select ⎰ German 1.. (3)
one ⎱ French 1.. (3)
Physics 1, General Course...................................... (3)
Physics 4, Electricity and Magnetism...................... (2)
Chemistry 3, Qualitative Analysis........................... (2)

JUNIOR YEAR

Mathematics 3, Surveying...................................... (2)
Mathematics 3B.. (2)
Mathematics 4.. (3)
Physics 4A, Electric Machinery............................... (2)
Physics 6, Thermodynamics.................................... (2)
Physics 11, Steam Machinery.................................. (2)
Drawing 2.. (2)

SENIOR YEAR

Physics 7, Alternating Currents............................... (4)
Physics 8, Batteries.. (1)
Physics 9, Electric Lighting, Wiring, and Distribution.......... (1)
Physics 10, Electric Testing.................................... (3)
Chemistry 7B, Electro-Chemistry.. .... (2)
Physics 12, Electrical Design.................................. (2)
Drawing 3.. (2)

III CIVIL ENGINEERING

FRESHMAN YEAR

English 1.. (3)
Mathematics 1.. (4)
Select ⎰ German 1.. (3)
one ⎱ French 1.. (3)
Chemistry 1.. (3)
Drawing 1.. (2)

SOPHOMORE YEAR

English 2 .... (3)
Mathematics 2 .... (3)
Mathematics 3, Surveying.. (2)
Mathematics 3A... (3)
Physics 1, General Course .... (3)
Drawing 2A.. (2)

JUNIOR YEAR

Mathematics 3B, Descriptive Geometry.. (2)
Mathematics 4, Calculus and Analytical Mechanics............................ (3)
Mathematics 7, Road and Railroad Surveying and Engineering (3)
Mathematics 16, Road Construction, Drainage, and Location (2)
English 3A.. ($1\frac{1}{2}$)
Geology 8A, Soil Surveying and Rocks for Road Construction (1)
Drawing 2.. (2)

SENIOR YEAR

Mathematics 7A, Hydraulics... (2)
Mathematics 11, Arches, Dams, and Sanitary Engineering..... (2)
Mathematics 8, Mechanics of Materials.. (3)
Mathematics 10, Stresses in Bridge and Roof Trusses.......... (4)
Mathematics 13, Design of Structures.. (2)
Physics 4A, Electrical Machinery.. (2)

IIIA. ROAD ENGINEERING

FRESHMAN YEAR

English 1... (3)
Mathematics 1.. (4)
Select { German 1.. (3)
one { French 1 .... (3)
Chemistry 1... (3)
Drawing 1.. (2)

SOPHOMORE YEAR

English 2.. (3)
Mathematics 2.. (3)
Mathematics 3.. (2)
Mathematics 3A... (3)
Physics 1.. (3)
Drawing 2A... (2)

JUNIOR YEAR

Mathematics 4, Calculus and Analytical Mechanics............ (3)
Mathematics 7, Road and Railroad Surveying and Engineering (3)
Mathematics 14, Brief course in Strength of Materials and
    Stresses in Trusses... (2)
Mathematics 16, Road Construction, Drainage, and Location (2)
Road Management, Building Model Roads........................ (1)
Geology 8A, Soil Survey and Rocks for Road Construction (1)
Drawing 2.. (2)
English 3A... ($1\frac{1}{2}$)

IV. MINING ENGINEERING

FRESHMAN YEAR

English 1.. (3)
German 1 .... (3)
Mathematics 1.. (4)
Chemistry 1, General Chemistry.................................... (3)
Drawing 1.. (2)

SOPHOMORE YEAR

English 2.. (3)
Mathematics 2.. (3)
Physics 1, General Course... (3)
Geology 1.. (3)
Chemistry 3, Qualitative Analysis................................. (2)
Drawing 2A... (2)

JUNIOR YEAR

Mathematics 3, Surveying and Leveling................. (2)
Mathematics 4, Calculus and Analytical Mechanics........ (3)
Physics 6, Thermodynamics and Steam Engine .... (3)
Geology 2, Mineralogy.............................. (3)
Chemistry 4, Quantitative Analysis.................... (3)
Geology 11, Ore Deposits............................ (1)
English 3A.. (1½)

SENIOR YEAR

Chemistry 2, Technical Chemistry, Metallurgy.... ...... (3)
Geology 4, Economic Geology......................... (3)
Geology 6, Mine Examinations........................ (3)
Geology 12, Principles of Mining.... .... (1)
Physics 4A, Electric Machinery....................... (2)
Mathematics 7A, Hydraulics.......................... (3)
Elective... (1)

V. SOIL INVESTIGATION

FRESHMAN YEAR

English 1.. (3)
Mathematics 1...................................... (4)
German 1.. (3)
Chemistry 1.. (3)
Drawing 1.. (2)

SOPHOMORE YEAR

English 2.. (3)
Mathematics 3...................................... (2)
Chemistry 3.. (2)
Geology 1.. (3)
Physics 1.. (3)
Drawing 2.. (2)

JUNIOR YEAR

Chemistry 4.................................. .... (3)
Geology 2 .... (3)
Botany 1... (3)
Chemistry 2... (3)
English 3A... (1½)
French 1... (3)

SENIOR YEAR

Geology 6... (3)
Geology 7.. (3)
Geology 8.. (3)
Chemistry 8.. (5)
Soils of the United States.......................... (1½)
Mapping.. (2)

COURSES OF INSTRUCTION

Only those scientific and language courses which are specifically required in the School of Applied Science are repeated here. For complete description of other courses, see pages 41ff. of general catalogue.

DEPARTMENT OF ENGLISH

Associate Professors McKie and Booker, Messrs. Grainger, Alexander, and Howard.

1. Types of literature: the short story, the novel, the essay, and the oration; the lyric, the epic, the ballad, and the drama. This course lays the foundation for the student's later studies in both literature and composition. The aim of the course is to inspire an appreciation of good literature by an intensive study of representative types. Practice in composition will be based chiefly upon the texts read. Required of Freshmen. *Both terms, three hours.*

Associate Professor Royster, Messrs. Grainger, Alexander, and Howard.

2. First term: Rhetoric and Composition; preparation and criticism of daily and weekly themes. Second term: History of English Literature. Reports on assigned readings. Manly's *English Poetry.* Required of Sophomores. *Both terms, three hours.*

Professor Graham.

3A. Composition: a practical course in expository writing designed to teach clearness and good construction. Lectures and theses. Required of Juniors in Courses III., IIIA., IV., V. *Fall term, three hours.*

DEPARTMENT OF ROMANCE LANGUAGES

Professor DEY, Associate Professor TOWLES, and Mr. VERMONT.

A. Elementary Course: grammar; careful attention to pronunciation; oral and written exercises; translation and reading at sight. This course may be counted for entrance only. *Both terms, three hours.*

1. Continuation of course A. Grammar; composition; reading of modern French literature. Freshman elective in Courses II., III., and III A. *Both terms, three hours.*

DEPARTMENT OF GERMANIC LANGUAGES

Professor TOY, Associate Professor COBB, and Mr. WINSLOW.

A. Elementary Course; grammar; written and oral exercises; translation; sight reading. This course may be counted for entrance only. *Both terms, three hours.*

Professor TOY and Associate Professor COBB.

1. Translation, sight reading, composition, grammar. Required of Freshmen in Courses I., IV., and V.; elective in Courses II., III., and III A. *Both terms, three hours.*

DEPARTMENT OF MATHEMATICS

Professor HENDERSON and Messrs. HICKERSON, HINES, and COSTNER.

1. Algebra, from Quadratics through Theory of Equations (Fine's *College Algebra*); Plane and Spherical Trigonometry and Logarithms. Required of Freshmen. *Both terms, four hours.*

Professors CAIN and HENDERSON.

2. Brief course in Conic Sections (Smith and Gale's *Analytic Geometry*); Elementary course in Differential and Integral Calculus (Cain's *Brief Course in the Calculus*). Required of Sophomores. *Both terms, three hours.*

Associate Professors STACY and MITCHELL.

3. (*a*) Surveying (Raymond), and (*b*)Higher Surveying. Required of Sophomores in Courses III., III A., and V., and of Juniors in Courses II. and IV. *Both terms, three hours.*

Professor HENDERSON.

3A. (*a*) Elementary Mechanics (Loney), (*b*) Higher Algebra. Required of Sophomores in Courses III., and III A. *Both terms, three hours.*

Associate Professor MITCHELL.

3B. Graphics: Descriptive Geometry (Church); Shades, Shadows, and Perspective (Mitchell). Required of Juniors in Courses II. and III. *Both terms, three hours.*

Professor CAIN.

4. Calculus, Analytic Mechanics. Required of Juniors in Courses II., III., III A., and IV.; prerequisite, Mathematics 2. *Both terms, three hours.*

Professor HENDERSON.

5. Theory of Equations (Burnside and Panton). Prerequisite, Mathematics 2. *Both terms, three hours.*

6. Differential Equations (Murray). Prerequisite, Mathematics 4. *Both terms, three hours.*

Associate Professor STACY.

7. Railroad Surveying and Railroad Engineering. Required of Juniors in Courses III. and III A.; prerequisite, Mathematics 3. *Both terms, three hours.*

7A. Hydraulics. Required of Seniors in Courses III. and IV.; prerequisite, Mathematics 4. *Both terms, two hours.*

Professor CAIN.

8. Mechanics of Materials. Required of Seniors in Course III.; prerequisite, Mathematics 4. *Both terms, three hours.*

Associate Professor STACY.

10. Stresses in Bridges and Roof Trusses, Graphical Statics. Required of Seniors in Course III.; prerequisite, Mathematics 4. *Both terms, four hours.*

Professor CAIN.

11. Arches, Dams, and Sanitary Engineering. Required of Seniors in Course III.; prerequisite Mathematics 4. *Both terms, two hours.*

Mr. HICKERSON.

13. Design of Structures. Required of Seniors in Course III.; prerequisite, fall term of Mathematics 8 and 10. *Spring term, four hours.*

14. Brief course in Strength of Materials and Stresses and Trusses. Required of Juniors in Course III A.; prerequisite, Mathematics 4. *Both terms, two hours.*

Associate Professor STACY.

16. Road Construction and Drainage; Road Location. Required of Juniors in Courses III. and III A. *Both terms, two hours.*

Drawing

Associate Professor MITCHELL.

1. Freehand Drawing and Mechanical Drawing; (*a*) freehand: pencil outline, pencil shading from the flat models and casts; (*b*) mechanical: use of instruments; geometrical constructions; freehand lettering; dimensioning; (*c*) plotting. Required of Freshmen. *Both terms, two hours.*

2. Mechanical and Topographical Drawing. (*a*) Orthographic projection; intersections; developments. (*b*) Machine drafting, conventional signs for materials of construction, sketching of machine details. (*c*) A course in tinting.

(d) Topography: conventional signs; hill shading; mapping. Required of Sophomores in course V., and of Juniors in Courses II., III., and III A. *Both terms, two hours.*

2A. Continuation of Drawing 1. Required of Sophomores in Courses I., III., and III A. *Both terms, two hours.*

3. Mechanical Drawing: machine drafting, work drawings; tracing and blue prints of machine details; assembly drawing; machine design; complete shop and erection drawing with bill of material, in accordance with modern drafting room systems and standards. Required of Seniors in Course II.; prerequisite, Drawing 1 and 2. *Both terms, two hours.*

DEPARTMENT OF PHYSICS

Professor PATTERSON.

1. General Physics: lectures, with text-book; problems; laboratory work. Required of Sophomores; prerequisite, Mathematics 1. *Both terms, three hours.*
Laboratory fee, $2.50 a session.

4. Study of Electricity and Magnetism, with laboratory work; Franklin and MacNutt's *Electricity and Magnetism.* Required of Sophomores in Course II. *Both terms, two hours.*
Laboratory fee, $4.00 a session.

Professor LATTA.

4A. Electrical Machinery; theory and practical operation of direct and alternating current dynamos and motors; testing of typical forms in the laboratory. Required of Juniors in Course II., and of Seniors in Courses I., III, and IV; prerequisite, Physics 1 and 4. *Both terms, two hours.*
Laboratory fee, $4.00 a session.

Professors PATTERSON and LATTA.

6. Advanced Heat and Thermodynamics. This study is based on Edser's *Heat for Advanced Students*, Ewing's *The Steam*

Engine and Other Heat Engines, and Peabody's *Thermodynamics of the Steam Engine.* Required of Juniors in Courses II. and IV., and of Seniors in Course I.; prerequisite, Physics 1. *Both terms, two hours.*

Professor LATTA.

7. Alternating Currents and Alternating Current Machinery; lectures and problem work; testing and study of alternating current machines in the laboratory. Required of Seniors in Course II.; prerequisite Physics 1 and 4A. *Both terms, four hours.*
   Laboratory fee, $5.00 a session.

8. Primary and Secondary Batteries. Required of Seniors in Course II.; prerequisite, Physics 1 and Chemistry 1. *Fall term, two hours.*

9. Electric Lighting, Wiring, and Distribution: a study of circuits for light and power. Required of Seniors in Course II.; prerequisite, fall term of Physics 7. *Spring term, two hours.*

10. Electric Testing: experimental study of electrical machinery and other apparatus. Required of Seniors in Course II.; prerequisite, Physics 4A. *Both terms, three hours.*
    Laboratory fee, $10.00 a session.

11. Steam Engineering: steam engines, steam turbines; gas engines, gas producers, gasoline engines, and other heat engines; steam boilers, steam pumps, and other boiler room accessories. Lectures, problems, and laboratory work. Required of Juniors in Course II.; prerequisite, Drawing 1 and Physics 6. *Both terms, two hours.*

12. Electric Design: design of electric machinery. Lectures, calculations, preparation of drawings and specifications. Required of Seniors in Course II.; prerequisite, Physics 7 and 10. *Spring term, two hours.*

DEPARTMENT OF CHEMISTRY

Professor HERTY and Mr. HILL.

1. General Descriptive Chemistry: a study of the elements and their compounds, including an introduction to Organic Chemistry; lectures with laboratory work. Required of Freshmen. *Both terms, three hours.*
   Laboratory fee: $1.25 a term.

Professor HERTY.

2. Technical Chemistry. (*a*) Industrial and Agricultural Chemistry: glass-making, acids, alkalies, phosphates, fertilizers, foods, clothing, hygiene, etc. (*b*) Metallurgy: mining, treatment of ores, smelting, chlorination, fuel, building materials, etc. Required of Juniors in Courses I. and V., and of Seniors in Course IV.; prerequisite, Chemistry 1. *Both terms, three hours.*

Associate Professor WHEELER and Messrs. OATES and TILLETT.

3. Qualitative Analysis; laboratory work with lectures. May be taken with Chemistry 1. Required of Sophomores in Courses I., II., IV., and V. *Both terms, two hours.*
   Laboratory fee, $5.00 a term.

Associate Professor MILLS.

4. Quantitative Analysis and Assaying; laboratory work, lectures, and stoichiometic exercises; a grounding in analytical methods. Required of Sophomores in Course I., and of Juniors in Courses IV. and V.; prerequisite, Chemistry 1 and 3. *Both terms, three hours.*
   Laboratory fee, $5.00 a term.

Associate Professor WHEELER.

5. Organic Chemistry. Required of Juniors in Course I.; prerequisite, Chemistry 1 and 3. *Both terms, three hours.*
   Laboratory fee, $4.00 a term.

5A. Organic Chemistry; special preparations. Required of Seniors in Course I. *Both terms, laboratory, two hours.*
Laboratory fee, $6.00 a term.

Associate Professor MILLS.

6. The Theories of Chemistry. Required of Seniors in Course I.; prerequisite, Chemistry 1, 3, 4, 5. *Both terms, two hours.*

7. Elementary Physical Chemistry. Required of Juniors in Course I.; prerequisite, Chemistry 1 and 3. *Both terms, three hours.*
Laboratory fee, $2.00 a term.

7A. Physical Chemistry; lectures and text-books, with laboratory work. Senior elective in Course I.; prerequisite, Chemistry 1 and 3. *Both terms, two hours.*

7B. Electro-Chemistry: theory and application of electricity to chemical processes. Senior elective in Course I.; prerequisite, Chemistry 1 and 3. *Both terms, two hours.*

Professor HERTY.

8. Quantitative Analysis; laboratory work; gas analysis and extension of course 4 in technical lines; bacteriological examination of water (with Professor MacNider); research. Required of Seniors in Course I.; prerequisite, Chemistry 1, 3, and 4. *Both terms, five hours.*
Laboratory fee, $10.00 a term.

16. Inorganic Chemistry. A detailed study of the reactions of the elements and their compounds. Lectures and text-book. Required of Juniors in Course I.; prerequisite, Chemistry 1. *Spring term, three hours.*

17. Quantitative Analysis. Laboratory work. Extension of course 4 in technical lines. Required of Juniors in Course I.; prerequisite, Chemistry 1, 3, and 4. *Both terms, three hours.*
Laboratory fee, $5.00 a term.

The Journal Club meets fortnightly. The current journals, American, English, German and French, both the purely scientific and the technical, are reviewed by the students and instructors. Attendance is expected of students in all courses except 1 and 3.

DEPARTMENT OF GEOLOGY AND MINERALOGY

Professor COBB aud Mr. FRY.

1. Elementary Geology; lectures with field work; laboratory work on the common minerals and rocks. Required of Sophomores in Courses IV. and V., and of Juniors in Course I. *Both terms, three hours.*

    Laboratory fee, $3.00 for the Spring term.

Mr. EATON.

2. Mineralogy: lectures with laboratory and field work; Crosby's *Tables* and Dana's *Text-book of Mineralogy*. Required of Juniors in Courses IV. and V., and of Seniors in Course I. *Both terms, three hours.*

    Laboratory fee. $5.00 a term.

4. Economic Geology: ore deposits and economic minerals; lectures with laboratory and field work. Required of Seniors in Course IV.; prerequisite, Geology 1 and Chemistry 1 and 3. *Both terms, three hours.*

Professor COBB.

6. Advanced field work and special research in Geology or Geography; problems and work adapted to the professional needs of the student. Students in this course are expected to keep Saturday open for field work. Required of Seniors in Courses IV. and V.; prerequisite, two courses in Geology. *Both terms, three hours.*

8. Origin and Nature of Soils; field work, laboratory, and theses. Students in this course are expected to keep Saturday open for field work. Required of Seniors in Course V. *Both terms, three hours.*

    Laboratory fee, $2.00 a term.

8A. Soils and Stones for Road Making. Field work, laboratory work. Required of Juniors in Courses III. and IIIA.; prerequisite, Geology 1. *Both terms, one hour.*

Laboratory fee, $1.00 a term.

Professor PRATT.

11. Mineral and Ore Deposits; lectures supplemented by laboratory and field work. Required of Juniors in Course IV. *Twenty-four lectures (spring term).*

12. Principles and Practice in General Mining; lectures supplemented by visits to different mining regions. Required of Seniors in Course IV.

The Geological Seminary meets fortnightly for review and discussion of current geological literature, and for the presentation of original papers.

Course in Soil Investigation

Professor COBB and Mr. HEARNE.

1. Agricultural Soils: an elementary course covering the nature, origin, and classification of soils, based on G. P. Merrill's *Rocks, Rock Weathering and Soils*, F. H. King's *The Soil*, and reports and bulletins of the Bureau of Soils, U. S. Department of Agriculture; lectures, reading, and field and laboratory work. Open to Juniors and Seniors. *Fall term, three hours.*

2. Soils of the United States: an introductory study of the chief soil provinces, soil series, and soil areas of the United States, with special reference to the soils of North Carolina. Required of Seniors in Course V. *Spring term, two hours.*

3. Soil Mapping: preparation of large scale soil maps of the Chapel Hill region. Required of Seniors in Course V. *Both terms, two hours.*

4. Soil Seminary: study of soil literature with preparation of reports on selected subjects. Open to students engaged in soil work. *One evening each week during February and March.*

LABORATORIES AND MUSEUMS

THE PHYSICAL LABORATORIES

ANDREW HENRY PATTERSON, A. M., DIRECTOR and *Professor of Physics*.

*JAMES EDWARD LATTA, A. M., *Professor of Electrical Engineering*.

THOMAS JOSEPH McMANIS, *Instructor in Physics*.

WILLIAM RUFUS EDMONDS, *Assistant in Physics*.

ALEXANDER LITTLEJOHN FEILD, *Assistant in Physics*.

JUNIUS SPAETH KOINER, JR., *Assistant in Physics*.

The Physical Laboratory occupies the eastern half of the main floor and almost the whole of the basement floor of the Alumni Building, amounting to about seven thousand feet of floor space.

The main floor is divided into two lecture rooms, an apparatus room, laboratory for students in the general course, Physics 1, and a laboratory for X-ray and photometric work.

In the rooms of the basement are located the gasoline engines, dynamos, motors, electrical laboratory, electric furnace, storage battery, and the workshop for wood and metal.

The Physical Laboratory is equipped with standard types of electrical machines: dynamos, motors, transformers, meters, switchboard, storage battery, electric furnace, and the accessories, needed for practical instruction in electrical engineering.

The electric light, central heating, and waterworks plants constitute valuable adjuncts to the laboratory. For work in practical testing there are available a 35 H. P. Ball engine, a 20 H. P. slide valve engine, two types of steam pumps, steam siphon, two gasoline engines, with calorimeters, meters, thermometers, and other accessory apparatus necessary for making complete tests on power plants. The central power plant of the University also contains a 115 H. P. Ball and Wood engine, directly connected to a Crocker-Wheeler 3-phase generator; a 70 H. P. Skinner engine

*Resigned, January, 1910.

with directly connected general electric generator; a De Laval Steam Turbine; a D'Oliver turbine pump, and all necessary accessories.

CHEMISTRY HALL

CHARLES HOLMES HERTY, PH.D., DIRECTOR and *Smith Professor of General and Industrial Chemistry.*

ALVIN SAWYER WHEELER, PH.D., *Associate Professor of Organic Chemistry.*

JAMES EDWARD MILLS, PH.D., *Associate Professor of Physical Chemistry.*

*ROYALL OSCAR EUGENE DAVIS, PH.D., *Associate Professor of Chemistry.*

HAMPDEN HILL, S. B., *Iustructor in Chemistry.*

EUGENE JOSEPH NEWELL, A. B., *Fellow in Chemistry.*

ERNEST NOELL TILLETT, A. M., *Fellow in Chemistry.*

WILLIAM MERCER OATES, A. B., *Assistant in Chemistry.*

THOMAS PALMER NASH, JR., *Assistant in Chemistry.*

JOHN HILL WHARTON, *Assistant in Chemistry.*

The overcrowded condition of the laboratories and lecture room in Person Hall and the unsatisfactory ventilation of the laboratories made urgent the need for a larger and better arranged building for the Department of Chemistry. These facts, together with complete plans for a new building, were laid before the Legislature in 1905 and an appropriation of $50,000 asked. The appropriation was voted, and in a short while the work of construction was under way.

The new building, Chemistry Hall, is located east of Alumni Hall and north of the New East building, facing west. By the selection of this location good water pressure is assured for all of the laboratories in the building.

The outer walls are of salt and pepper brick laid with black mortar.

The main building, 120 x 68 x 48, comprises a first floor, a second floor, and a commodious basement. Adjoining this main

---

*Resigned, November, 1909.

building and to the rear of the centre is the lecture room, 41 x 62 x 22.

To the right on entering the main building are the office and the private laboratory of the Director, the department library, and a small lecture room; to the left are the office and private laboratory of the Associate Professor of Organic Chemistry, a large laboratory for organic chemistry, containing locker desks for twenty-four students, and a combustion room.

On the rear or east side of the first floor are the laboratories for quantitative analysis (thirty-two desks), and adjacent fume room, advanced quantitative analysis (twenty-four desks), and technical chemistry (six desks). At each end of the corridor are balance rooms.

On the second floor are the laboratories for general chemistry (sixty-six desks), qualitative analysis (sixty desks), physical chemistry (eight desks), electro-chemistry (eight desks), a research laboratory (sixteen desks), a laboratory for physiological chemistry (forty-eight desks), a fume room, and a small lecture room. At the ends of the corridor on the second floor are a balance room, preparation room, and a dark room for spectroscopic work.

In the basement are the assay laboratory, rooms for gas machine, electric furnace, technical chemistry, constant temperature, a photographic dark room, laboratory and museum for chemical mineralogy, a carpenter-shop, stock room for heavy chemicals, and a large stock room for chemicals and apparatus. From this stock room material is supplied to each floor of the building by an elevator.

Each laboratory is furnished with ample fume closets for the removal of noxious gases, while pivoted window sash insure proper ventilation of the rooms.

The entire building is heated by hot water from the central system of the University.

The main entrance hall leads direct to the lecture room, which is well lighted by high arched windows and has a seating capacity of two hundred, which can be increased somewhat as needs requires. To the rear of the lecture room are a preparation room and a museum for specimens of typical chemicals, mineral, and products illustrating the various phases of chemical industries. Above these two last rooms is a small room for filing charts, diagrams, etc., used in illustrating lectures.

THE BIOLOGICAL LABORATORY

HENRY VAN PETERS WILSON, PH.D., DIRECTOR and *Professor of Zoology*.
WILLIAM CHAMBERS COKER, PH.D., *Professor of Botany*.
HAL FULLERTON BOATWRIGHT, A. B., *Assistant in Zoology*.
ORREN WILLIAM HYMAN, *Assistant in Zoology*.
ELDEN BAYLEY, *Assistant in Botany*.

The Biological Laboratory, which bears the name of Davie Hall, is occupied by the Departments of Zoology and Botany. The building is a rectangular structure of pepper and salt brick and is divided into a main body and two wings. The total length is 125 feet, the depth of the main body 44 feet, that of the wings 38 feet. A basement underlies the whole, above which are two floors. The main body has an additional third floor which extends out over the wings forming spacious air chambers. The building faces north and south, lies to the east of the New East, and adjoins the Arboretum.

The entrance hall on the first floor, lit with large windows on either side of the main doorway, serves for the exhibition of museum specimens of a more popular character. Back of the entrance hall are herbarium, a room for charts and other lecture apparatus, and a room for the storage of zoological collections. The east wing of this floor is occupied by a lecture room with a seating capacity of one hundred and twenty, the west wing by a laboratory for the elementary classes in zoology and botany. The latter laboratory is arranged for twenty-four wall tables with window in front of each table.

On the second floor the east wing is occupied by a single large laboratory for advanced work in zoology and the west wing by a similar laboratory for advanced work in botany. Each of these rooms accomodates twenty workers and is lit on three sides with twenty windows. .The main building on this floor includes private work rooms for the professors of zoology and botany, two store rooms, and a library. On the third floor of the main body is a photographic studio with windows on the north side extending to the floor, and with sky-lights. The building is provided with electric lights and is heated with hot water. The furnace and fuel rooms are in the basement. Here also are fire proof incubator room, a room for micro-photography with adjoining dark room, janitor's shop, and rooms for the storage of heavy supplies. The wings in the basement are designed for the keeping of live animals and plants and for experimental work in botany and zoology. An elevator connects the basement with all floors.

THE GEOLOGICAL LABORATORY AND MUSEUM

COLLIER COBB, A. M., DIRECTOR and *Professor of Geology and Mineralogy.*

JOSEPH HYDE PRATT, PH.D., *State Geologist and Professor of Economic Geology.*

HARRY NELSON EATON, A. M., *Instructor in Geology.*

WILLIAM HENRY FRY, *Assistant in Geology.*

The Geological Laboratory occupies the first floor of the New East Building. In addition to a lecture room with a seating capacity of about ninety, there is a large laboratory supplied with working collections of minerals, rocks, and fossils, and with photographs, maps, and models illustrating geological structure. The laboratory is furnished with two petrographical microscopes, with microscopes for soil study, and with apparatus for the slicing and polishing of rocks. Microscope slides have been made of most of the specimens from North Carolina; and the department has, also, sections of the typical European rocks. Sections of the rocks around Chapel Hill, and the igneous rocks of the Boston Basin made by the late Hunter Lee Harris, of the class of 1889, were given to the geological department. There is a room for photographic work.

The University possesses a collection of more than two thousand specimens of building stones, coals, and various products illustrating the economic geology of the State.   These are arranged in an exhibition room of six hundred and fifty square feet of floor space. Here also are kept the sections taken with a diamond drill in the coal regions of Pennsylvania, in the region around King's Mountain, where the Summer School of Geology held its sessions, in the Dan River coal fields, and in the Triassic Rocks at Durham, N. C. A complete set of the ores of the precious metals found along the line of the Atchison, Topeka, and Santa Fe Railroad is included in the collection.   Valuable additions have been made to the collections of fossils also, affording increased opportunity for laboratory work in historical geology and palaeontology.   A small collection of tertiary type fossils from Florida, the gift of Mr. Joseph Wilcox of Philadelphia, is the most recent addition to the palaeontological collection.   The collection illustrating economic geology has been largely increased.

The department library, which occupies a room adjoining the exhibition room, is supplied with State and United States Reports, the papers of working geologists, the best works upon Geology, and scientific periodicals.

THE UNIVERSITY

OF

)RTH CAROLINA

THE ONE HUNDRED AND
FIFTEENTH SESSION

HE

PUBLISHED BY THE UNIVE...
CHAPEL HILL